Grasp Fire

Mathew Michael Collins

Published by Mathew Michael Collins, 2017 www.graspfire.com

© 2017, Grasp Fire All rights reserved. Copyrights for individual works rest with the respective contributors. No part of this book, either in part or in whole, may be reproduced, modified, stored in a retrieval system, transmitted or utilized, in any form or by any means, electronic, mechanical or otherwise, without prior permission from the Publisher, except for brief quotations embodied in literary articles and reviews.

All fear the Poet's Curse

First Edition, Walpurgisnacht 2017

ISBN # 978-0-692-88010-4

All poems and editing thereof by Mathew Michael Collins

Concept cover art by Sam Wilcox (Chosenundead117@gmail.com)

Concept art for Grasp Fire logo by Ahl (pandaking757@yahoo.com)

Graphic designer: Boris Dechovski (Decovski @ fiverr.com)

Copies may be ordered from graspfire.com or most fine retailers through the distributor Ingram Spark

Introduction

Elder ones

who came before,

that paved the way

for me,

a door.

May it never close,

either side,

to you

I raise a horn

ever to confide!

Grasp Fire

Table of Contents

A toast 1

Alibi 3

All In 5

All Secrets Whispered 7

Ashes 11

Atone 14

Battlefield 16

Black Puddle 19

Blinds 22

Close to You 25

Coming Home 27

Consume Me 29

Contrast 31

Could I 34

Deal with It 36

Death a Reason to Live 39

Disperse 42

Eternal Suffering 44

Ever No Light 47

Familiar Darkness 50

First Time Stung 52

Fog Abyss 55

Found 58

Four Aces 61

Glimpse 64

Golden Delight 66

Good 'til the Last Drop 68

Half-Wild 70

Haunted Shell 73

How 76

Idly Masturbate 78

Journey Through the Wild 81

Like Sand 85

Maiden Voyage 88

Memories 89

Moonless Tide 91

More 93

Myself 95

No Longer Say 98

Not Enough 100

Nowhere Left 102

Only the Ones That Knew 104

Pollen 108

Program 110

Rome Burning 113

Shedding Human Masks 118

Sleep Again 121

Sound 123

Suspended in the Sea 125

Sway 127

Tender Middle 130

The Rest 132

They're There 135

Too Long Denied 138

Trapped 140

Wake Up 142

Where 144

Wisdom 147

With It You 149

Without a Sound 153

Worse Before Better 154

Ye Who Enter 157

Zombie 159

A Toast

Chasing, chasing

of the ghosts,

fire my heart,

evil, my host,

out of the ashes,

into the grave.

A toast, we'll say a toast!

To the dead, and to the ghosts!

Chase them, chase them

into mind,

original place, them, to find.

Drive them, drive them

from the field,

glowing with powers,

that they wield.

Deeper, deeper,

still, the night,

silent to most,

remains out of sight.

Out of sight, out of mind,

how indeed did I find?

The ghosts I know,

behind the line,

if there remain,

I wouldn't mind,

but they jump,

from place to place,

trying on masks,

masks of my face,

back into place.

I cannot erase,

they never betray,

kinder word, to you, I say!

Alibi

What to do when old friends leave?

Where to go when their face haunts?

Lock the door,

windows shut,

voices still taunt,

from some faraway place,

right nearby,

caught red-handed,

without an alibi.

They don't leave,

no matter

how many tears

we cry.

Missed so much,

gone forever?

Only energy,

none of us here.

Don't forget to live each moment,

caught in time.

Live every second, don't regret,

wake up, breathe the air,

let it fill your being,

live like it's your first day here!

Like there never will be a worst day,

like you've got something to say!

All In

Go all in,

ante up.

No pieces to play,

a busted chump.

Thrill,

nervousness,

a reason to play,

more important

than winning, some say.

No drive,

stagnation;

not alive,

standing ovation.

Disappear,

if withdrawn,

no dice,

if you're here,

not gone.

Gleam in the eye,

don't lose it.

Lust, for the game,

chase

not fame,

but want,

the reason we play.

All Secrets Whispered

Lay my head,

to Mother Earth,

and hear,

all secrets whispered,

into my ear.

You know nothing,

until you know all,

ever close to me,

the ones that did fall.

In trees, they reside,

near me, in sleep,

in silence, like stones,

but at night, they weep.

Dance around

from the ground,

like fairies,

trumpet,

from them,

what sound, resound.

Golden fleece,

on bloody knees,

stare into the void,

see the secrets it keeps.

Bees, bats, birds, abyss,

locked into Nature's kiss.

Exposing her fangs,

entangled embrace,

'round and 'round trees,

always, chase.

Sisyphus ever pushing,

boulder up the hill,

every night,

what resilient will!

She tenderly molests,

concealed from me, destiny.

Parts, pieces,

like puzzle,

revealed,

escape,

from ancient tomb,

sealed.

Back from the dead,

again,

once more,

stare into great beauty,

I so adore.

Into the lake,

into the shore,

have it all,

yet I crave more!

Set in stone,

I break no bone,

I wish I could reveal,

secrets to me, shown,

but to you, until found,

on your own, unknown

shall they stay,

until you find them,

one glorious day!

Ashes

On my door,

the beast pounds,

his breath, hideous,

none hear sounds,

deep in nocturnal hours;

never, headstone,

nor grave flowers.

Straight from the ground,

myself,

they've taken;

my brains,

organs,

heart and soul, forsaken.

Doomed never to die,

yet, to forever live

in the pain of death.

Never shall I rest in peace.

Dug up from the grave,

before in the ground,

I lay.

A Daemon's will,

in ancient tongues,

many curses said.

For in darkness,

gloom it harkens,

to where my soul,

my heart,

as if Robin Hood,

as grim reaper should,

took apart,

given to the poor,

now eternally,

I am nothing,

nothing more.

Sullen, in sorrow,

no soul

left to borrow.

My eyes, forever,

embedded

in tears of flames,

ash.

Atone

The truth,

thrown aside,

rules to which,

we don't abide,

can't ignore Daemon,

need a ride?

Death, unaccounted for,

on pale horse,

take flight!

Blackness, the poison,

in which we inhale,

the wind in our sail,

life gives us power,

with which to fight back.

Rattlesnake gives me a break,

harsher words for me to take,

ones I won't soon forsake.

Clouds swirl, breasts squeezed,

mirror seized and silent,

breath takes and snakes,

for, dew's companion,

apprentice of darkness and light,

new taker of life,

have these words bestowed upon you:

Hate, Love

Ancient Egypt

1934

In Stone

Atone

Battlefield

Not that I don't want to live,

the choice,

taken away.

Skeletons of the dead

cover my mouth,

for lack of words to spout.

Horror entices,

Death invites,

finally a welcoming hand!

For all others,

cold and distant,

I want to go,

yet my spirit, resistant.

When Death comes knocking,

you answer.

Ancient battlefield,

my evil soul never fled,

technically, was I born,

if I never left the dead?

Cemetery comfort,

mournful ability to breathe,

yet, stillbirth,

I've been dead,

and any breath,

I've failed to retrieve.

Pure evil, or the will to live,

it's your choice,

which label you give.

Lake of blood, calls to me,

I hear her in the wind,

I feel me in the flames.

Words unspoken

by the living,

yet I understood,

more than I ever could.

Black Puddle

Little black puddle,

nothing less,

nothing more,

of my existence,

unaware.

Invisibly sneak

into the room,

not a head turns,

but entered

into your mind,

what secrets learned.

Mazes of caverns,

of Pharaohs,

O', kings,

fiery bird,

bringer of knowledge,

O', what songs does sing.

Take you away,

far away,

familiar place,

never been,

drifting back,

toward yourself,

to see as never seen.

Awake, and alive,

in your blood, I do thrive,

on your blood, does feed,

fulfilling need.

Darkness falls, like a shroud,

I gleam, nocturnally,

in the sky, not a cloud.

Without shame, fear,

without fame,

though ever near.

Creative, destructive,

connective, seductive,

alive.

O', little black puddle.

Blinds

Away, away with the blinds,

back into graven mind,

back, back before there's time,

again, with song,

again, with rhyme.

Celebration, celebration,

I must bring the feast.

Deep, deep inside my brain,

I let go the beast.

Frozen solid, cracked ice,

hold sway with luck,

old fool,

roll the dice.

All a fool has is luck,

all a fool has is luck,

but if shall save,

me from my plight,

again, I peer,

back into sight.

Open the shades,

my mind's betrayed,

seven of hearts,

and the Ace of spades.

Darkness, darkness,

again, shall pass,

how long, shall last?

The ghosts that come,

ghastly ghoul,

a fool,

not an ass,

unicorn,

not a mule.

Make haste,

tormenting tests,

let life be filled

with big natural breasts.

Tests, tests of the mind,

one must see white,

before closing blinds.

Close to You

Darkest cave.

You only know

what you feel,

what you think,

what is true?

Light that beckons,

or inner darkness?

You're not confused,

it's light you've viewed,

but why travel

so far in the dark?

Pitch black construed.

Your heart aches for what's lurking

in darkest corners.

You feel pride for the light you find.

True light can only be seen in dark places,

so, to the darkest place,

you've come,

to reveal to yourself true light,

from within your own self,

and from within me.

Feel my presence, like thunder.

I'm deep within you,

in your mind.

I am you,

your mirror image.

Imagine now,

let yourself free,

immerse yourself in the dark,

yet hold the light close,

close to you.

Coming Home

Selfishly I await,

as if I, again should rise,

10,000 feet above lifted,

still not enough high,

above to lift me,

over the lies.

So I'm off, I'm beaten,

defeated in two,

disappeared out of view.

Ashamed of my own being,

hiding myself in a box,

ashamed to have ever lived,

this reality of me,

forever mocks.

I'm retreating, giving in,

surrendering six feet of ground,

never again, a sound.

Goodnight now.

Into dreams, receding,

not even onto other realms,

just gone, vanquished,

left to haunt.

A carrion amidst turmoil,

body gone, into soil.

Face, eaten away,

blue and cold,

no life left.

I have no more of life,

the gift.

I'm coming home.

Consume Me

Illusions obstruct,

cut deep into what is.

Dive blindly, frozen lake,

black, as clear,

depth unknown,

swallowed whole.

Bright lights adorn my face,

attachments of the human race,

colours bleed off canvas,

the only reality.

Our pulse, nature.

Connected, but what to?

Stars circle, mockingly.

Your whole life,

as one day, viewed.

Invaders tie you down,

served as pie,

epitome of gluttony,

all-encompassing void.

Brightest capacity,

bulb, orb, bud.

Frosty, murky surface,

deceptive at its core,

non-existent,

deepest, blackest depths.

Jaws of hideous monster,

consume me.

Contrast

Darkest abyss,

brightest of lights,

from the depths,

angels and bats,

dead of night.

Fearless encounter

realization sets in.

You, a guest,

and the main course.

You are being had,

dinner bell rings,

toll from beyond.

A chill up your spine,

fangs drawn.

From out of coffin,

to prowling street,

wasp doesn't die,

after initial sting.

Two puncture wounds,

only evidence.

Crime to be food chain's top,

or mortal jealousy,

immortal's crop?

Every man's dream,

to never meet death,

meet your maker soon.

Pulled by horses,

ancient chariot,

the count races,

against the sun,

but just like Pan,

against Apollo,

this battle shall never be won.

How could a vampyre's tale,

not end most tragic?

Their existence,

to end others' lives.

A fairytale ending,

did you really expect,

when doomed from beginning?

Could I

Always uninvited,

one with shadows,

in darkness, united.

I, familiar face,

none seem to know,

standing out,

never out of place.

Did you see me?

Always doubt.

As I walk by,

wind, not still,

an unexpected shiver,

up your spine,

a chill.

My face solemn, yet bold;

windows are closed,

yet I bring in the cold.

Familiar,

as repetitious dream,

strange, lingering deja-vu,

yet more a nightmare,

it would seem.

Not all have spotted me.

Could I be a ghost?

Could I be a ghost?

Deal with It

Everyone waves

the flag, proudly,

knowing we all,

in a cloud, of mist,

exist.

Is it still

considered a lie,

if the truth

has someone's twist?

I am American,

proud as all red, white, and blue,

to blindly be asked,

for a lie to be followed,

how highly, one thinks of you?

Devil behind the giant,

for them, so eager to die,

yet not enough tears

for the sorrow to be shed,

for those, lost in the desert;

how blindly the reasons,

the lies, they were lead.

How easy it is to trick a child,

faded into the long mile.

Forgotten, silenced,

are his woes,

as in shackles

father, brother, and sister goes.

Forget the dead,

they may as well say,

for none of the blood is lost,

from which is of their own.

Houses torn apart, can't compete,

with so many new homes

which they've littered the street.

Eaten out of house and home,

to pay taxes

for the bum and whore,

we'll bend over,

again, and again.

Hypocrites will drown

in their own shit,

then, how will they deal with it?

Death, a Reason to Live

Death rides,

a darkened course.

On, and on, and on,

never stopping, from beyond.

Ever, just out of sight,

begin or end, to joyous delight?

Fiery charcoal, eyeless eyes,

Death never ceases,

ever rides.

Marching out on horseback,

always, seeks a soul.

Death, no mercy, discrimination,

coming, with hesitation.

Hang on tight, to that dear life,

yet a never-winning battle.

Darkness, grey mist, fog,

ever peering, yet I am fond.

What in shadows lie,

to stir the hearts of man?

Ever trickster, good ol' Pan.

Just fear in mind,

pandemonium strikes.

Ever-fruitful Earth,

bearing nectar, ambrosia.

Indulge thyself,

live every moment.

Never to know, Death appears.

Be not prepared, be not worried!

Live, live, live,

that's what the dead would say,

if they could have but one more day!

Death shall not be scary,

but a friend, never an end.

Too much mourning,

beckons once more.

Tempt not, lest ye want,

suggested instead, to just live,

forever, again and again if ye wish!

Disperse

Fear, so beloved,

little child.

In love with fear itself.

In need of dog guardian,

to protect thine soul.

Born from the wild,

more special than mild;

lost in the dark, seek what's bright,

entangled with the little light.

Peering in pits, utter darkness,

if you knew how far down

in the depths, you play,

you would disperse,

but your surroundings to you,

remain unknown.

Unsettled,

in your comfort,

craving for the dark,

unaware, your desire,

through shadows,

haunt.

You can't see,

how did you end up here?

Follow instincts blindly,

follow your heart,

seeking light in the dark.

Unclear,

yet, full of light,

that you think you want,

then why in darkness,

do you tread?

Eternal Suffering

Nothing,

will overthrow my will!

My body, dying not,

the thing I longed for,

yet never got.

My face, in mirror,

cracked,

all the things,

I've ever lacked.

From disturbed mind,

created,

the crimes, unwillingly abated.

Speak in tongues,

bark of flame,

all this training,

still, remain untamed.

Death beckons us all,

yet I dance to his call,

never to fall.

Aeterno,

Gollum and his precious one ring.

Just a nightmare,

soon to wake,

how much more,

sleep can I take?

Hypnos shall decide,

if I shall subside,

next to me, in my coffin.

Seven-layered mask,

999 years to accomplish

enduring task.

Tragic comedy,

a clown's tale,

nothing can cure my sickness,

not even ale.

Yet I shall keep trying,

perhaps to fail,

definition of crazy,

repetition,

whenever I doubt,

unsure of the reality

that I've sought out.

Ever, No Light

There is a place,

deep inside,

frightening redefined.

A place,

you wouldn't want

to be alone.

Deep in mind,

your eye,

you can travel to,

you can go,

but a path,

none can show.

What lies inside,

forever,

changes.

What lies inside,

dead,

yet reaches still.

From darkest corner,

of room, pitch black,

grasping for you.

Once you see them,

quiet panic.

Once you can't,

fear strikes.

Once they've grabbed you,

too late,

no turning back,

in the dead of night.

Once the dead

have you

in sight,

you've gone

to the other side.

Parody, tragedy,

wrapped in one.

Forever in darkness,

ever, with no light.

Familiar Darkness

Shooting star,

wishing afar,

never knowing,

just what you are,

ever to wonder,

in cold, dark night.

I am alone,

at home,

feel the wind, brush against

my other self, I've sensed.

I must be low,

I don't even know.

Myself

back together again,

can the Fates ever sew?

Destined to be,

burning out,

yet ever ablaze,

lost again,

out in space.

When alone,

what to measure

yourself against?

Have I become,

dark and desolate?

For space, all I know,

always alone,

alone, in cold space,

darkness to me,

my familiar.

First Time Stung

Re-entered life

pulse, electrified.

Resurgence in my veins,

beckons a call,

I answer, triumphantly!

O', glorious day it is,

to rise,

throughout, revitalized.

When life seems

to fade,

upon awakening,

life's parade!

A friend's remembrance,

many winters gone,

as if to sing,

nearly-forgotten song.

To awaken on a crisp morn,

such a gift;

to awaken once more,

what a lift.

O', for life, so much to offer,

just when thought,

I know it all,

comes tearing down

of a giant wall,

perception,

when breaketh away,

reveals,

such marvel,

unknown.

As if old songs,

first time, sung,

as if by hornet,

first time, stung.

Fog Abyss

Darkness surround,

shrouded,

lost in stride,

nocturnal.

Clouds thunder,

deep in my chasm.

I necromance those parts,

running the great race,

longest to last.

Spirit animal, strong, wise,

guide me on my path;

enemies tremble before me,

thou shalt fear my wrath!

A whirlwind,

dark ancient magic,

life consumed,

strong forces,

torn asunder,

patched together.

Spiral into the void,

within fog abyss,

stirring, churning cauldron

bring me bliss.

Add an herb,

an ancient word,

fly by night, like a bird.

Wizard Poet Warrior Hero,

appear before me.

In all your grandeur, shine.

Inspired by the Phoenix,

fire magic power,

time exists not,

lost within the hour.

Merlin, bats, owls,

black cats, coyotes, wolves,

serpents, magic,

sacred, olde, spirits bold!

Moonlight, from twilight,

cloud cover, dark,

wolves howling,

from night, stark!

Wild,

free at last.

Released death grip,

never shall slip,

hold grasp infinitely.

Figure eight,

relate,

Celtic knot, invigorate!

Fairies, tree nymphs,

dance around!

Found

Stoned, I sit,

sacred herb,

delicious garden.

Death, pale,

frightened in the night.

Long too long,

you're dead too,

but what is death?

Certainty,

fear,

the end,

of another beginning.

Unknown to all?

Some?

Maybe they're better off

not knowing

what lies beyond,

or maybe they can't,

different for all.

What do I know?

Nothing,

or everything,

which is witch?

Unwind the snake,

down a tainted valley,

poison.

Walk,

alone,

desperate loft.

Insane from

exhaustion,

and heat.

Lost in the desert,

in the desert, found.

Four Aces

It's not the heat,

which, to me, a burden,

but only what's bright;

there are some,

so full of sorrow,

that they never see the light.

To myself, forbidden,

on the boat,

across Styx, ridden;

from myself,

my soul and face

ever hidden.

Of me, there is no more,

disintegrated into ash.

Sorrow painfully,

grips my heart, black,

from this death,

can't turn back.

Yet, to my dismay,

there is not an end!

The shepherd is crippled and gone,

nothing did heaven send.

Looking back,

all, black,

smoke consumes,

what life once had,

my sorrowful fate, far beyond sad.

Rowing down, ever cursed,

on Styx to sail,

in what used to be my life,

ended, no winning,

nor have I failed.

Trapped in Pandora's box,

ripped from my socks,

no flesh is left,

only pain;

ever on me

blood shall rain.

There is no grace,

in which my body is held,

for four aces,

the hand I was dealt.

Glimpse

Stagnant,

motion.

Await a future

that may not be,

focus on the now.

To a silent cave,

reflect;

frost-bitten dew drop,

introspect.

I had to kill myself,

to wake up,

from recurring dream;

strangle all that's beautiful,

harder task

than it may seem.

I stare into my own eyes

in that glimpse,

I leapt, a chance.

All I needed,

freed from frost,

a necessary cost.

Embrace the pain

or it will engulf,

only then, exhume

worthwhile smoke.

I freed myself,

once I finally broke.

Golden Delight

In need of new means,

an insanity

more favourable to me.

Searching for secrets

in the stars,

knowledge before you,

but still, you travel far.

Float asunder,

always to wonder,

what the hell's really going on?

Has everyone else

vacated their bodies?

Tired of it,

So, they've just

picked up and gone?

O', I need to relax,

with a golden song,

hear the voice of the Phoenix,

feel the untamed lynx.

What of deja-vu?

What of jinx?

Enter subconscious,

traveling body of light,

in dark

corners of my mind.

Traveling, body out of sight,

to seek out a truth,

golden delight.

Good 'Til the Last Drop

I am water, I am tide,

I am Earth, unbound,

I'm death, beyond death,

before and after death,

yet, so much left.

I am the breath of fire

which doth caress, sweet desire.

I, the cold breath on your neck,

in the cold dark.

Unwatched, un-protested,

unacknowledged, unmolested.

I, the omni-present,

I, the one,

but why defy, if not for fun?

Perhaps to never see the sun,

a deal in blood,

can't be undone.

Undying, eternal,

hungry for you,

veins pulsing every glance I take.

Must look away,

lest I not forsake.

Bloodlust.

A possession beyond physical,

the worst of addictions,

one which cannot be broken,

nor resisted.

Half-Wild

Where are you, Native child?

Half-animal, half-man wild.

Arising along,

rising of the tide,

always near

fire's side.

Appearing, moon full,

vision quest,

heart of bull.

Smoke whispers,

through the night,

fading in and out of sight;

Fate taught by weaving

spider webs,

children of the stars,

celestial midnight.

Aura rich and bright,

almost out of sight,

in the clear,

always near,

always here,

amidst sacred stones,

rocks and bones.

Night shows the way,

paved without hypocrisy,

without human guise,

begin to realize,

we have three eyes.

Dancing around,

arising much dust,

from out of the flames,

madness, and lust.

Vision quest, attempt to flee,

from what, should not be.

A test, what one's

mind and spirit could see.

What animal spirits did, to you, show?

Haunted Shell

In my later days,

unable to have a sun,

Gaze into mirror,

where I used to stand

realize not me,

staring back,

but cold-stone killer,

looking upon himself

as he finally dies.

Seems everywhere I look,

a ghost remains,

into this haunted shell,

my broken body contains,

stewed and tormented remains.

Cold rain falls this day,

what was once me,

has washed away.

Of the seasons,

no more viewed,

drank of this poison,

I'd construed,

and as

I'm washed away,

of all my wicked, wicked ways,

removed of all my evil days,

I look back upon myself

and am no more.

The children hear them too,

the ghosts that follow me,

know it's true.

The ghosts that are, also me,

haunt,

midnight,

awaken to taunt,

removed from me, my body.

After so much pain, bestowed,

sorrow, another name's begotten,

after too much sadness, made known,

all my days, crumbled now.

How

How has this been?

How can this be?

Is the man, in the mask,

is it really me?

I smoke, I smoke,

the more I smoke,

the more it's clear,

the more I keep on smoking,

I learn to disappear.

Fading, fading from this dream,

not quite as real

as I thought I seemed.

Waking, waking through the night,

everyone else fades out of sight,

I'm all I have left,

and I know it's not right.

Where did go mythological times,

which were mine only delight?

Enriching the seasons

with my body, I soil,

into the deepest flames, begot.

Bubble, bubble, burn, and boil,

deep beneath the ground,

O', nocturnal mole.

Idly Masturbate

Wondrous Voodoo trip,

from heaven's mantle, slip.

Reach inside

darkened heart,

already there,

can't recall start,

ripped apart.

All the shrunken heads,

things in mind,

what I dread.

Awaken, in this state,

to beautifully procreate,

or idly masturbate?

With left hand,

to have no worry,

evil to cut it off,

in righteous fury.

Frozen angel,

do I descend,

or am I climbing,

do I pretend?

It's all in your mind,

heightened awareness;

by the Gods,

how shall all bare this?

Tears of angels,

and their wings,

lured into rocks,

where sirens sing.

O', poor Odysseus!

Ears, tormented,

piercing shrill,

tied to mast,

shall surpass,

soul defended

such will!

Hard to believe,

to yourself,

hardest to deceive.

What black curse,

did you contrive?

Will my dark heart ever revive?

Journey Through the Wild

Buried,

in the woods.

A chance,

for freedom.

Reincarnation,

in most spectacular ways.

To fall,

by bear,

rise,

as tree;

where once

I was human,

inside wolf coyote.

Dancing rain,

around,

the fire,

circle calls.

Out of madness,

freedom,

found,

spinning 'round and 'round,

to the sounds,

to the sounds,

of the great triumph,

spirit,

grasp fire!

Hawk, eagle,

snake, lizard,

smoke signal

of my spirit,

set free,

as a tree,

with wood nymphs,

I am me,

Pan!

Clouds abound,

rain plummets,

but put out flame,

does not!

Ancient dreams,

of ancient ones,

descend into madness.

To find yourself,

lift off mask,

a scalping,

blood from palm,

to face.

Dancing around,

spirit dance,

of sacred elder children,

of the forest,

the wild,

the free.

I shall fall,

a man beast,

by paws, of bear,

and rise a tree,

without a care.

Like Sand

A new flavour of bland hit my tongue,

all lost hope,

sober song sung.

What more are we left to do?

Debt collectors here,

Death says it's due.

There's been a killer,

but you don't know who,

better watch out,

or be run through!

The weed is dry,

the empty bottle,

the smoke put out,

no lasses though.

Life has dried up,

exit the magic,

gather all around,

for news, most tragic.

My eyes can't see, what I don't believe,

they don't see much these days,

that which they do see

bleak, or prophetic in dream.

Spiral down, on back, behind

someone left on the rain,

can't see myself anymore,

forgot to plug the drain.

Skin melting away,

revealing chaos and disorder,

dead deer, death here,

take away, the pain.

Bright white pain, in death, relief,

wisdom sought,

which I seek.

Can't tell you the flavour,

lick my tongue,

see if it's hot,

if it sears or sheers,

or fades away, like sand on the tide.

Ride the night or get out of sight,

long as there's no fucking light.

Maiden Voyage

I shouldn't be here,

always in places,

I ought not see.

In those places,

reunited, memory.

Deja-vu,

for the maiden voyage.

Memories

When a hero falls,

it is not into darkness,

but like a star,

from the night,

ever bright.

Twinkling, then out of sight,

like the cold chill down your spine,

not losing your mind,

opening it.

No one ever leaves us,

don't leave them behind.

With hope, love, and memories,

we'll keep alive.

Their magic never left,

flame never dies,

dims momentarily,

only to rekindle,

again, and again.

The moment we think they're done,

burst into flame,

their eternal spark.

Everywhere are they

and maybe they will answer you,

if they have words to say...

Moonless Tide

Wanton eyes 'o gold,

taste of rum on lips,

not old,

not home on his soul, sold.

To fulfill his quest,

ever eager,

but long stories,

made in stride,

his lust for gold,

he couldn't hide,

for only by it and sea, did he abide.

Vessels adrift,

moonless tide,

Moon's on end,

but he'd never died.

Songs o' long,

songs o' old,

he'll fulfill his quest,

before his chest,

grows cold,

and empty.

O', for he was an old lost pirate soul,

he thirsts only for rum,

wants nothing save gold.

Poseidon, father of the sea,

ever-changing sway,

hold thee,

up and down,

tides rise and fall,

and so, to you,

we gave it all,

please accept our pirate offering.

More

How come the shadows,

ever moving?

Why burning fire,

still, so soothing?

Drinking, blinking,

life flashes before your eyes.

Not thinking on the brink,

death is no surprise.

Daemon's chalice,

suffering,

ancient palace,

calling me,

back down,

in the ground,

nature surrounds,

all around,

without a sound,

without resound.

Traces back, point of origin,

no start,

where to begin?

Must breathe before

inevitable end.

Missing pieces,

sounds like Hell,

will I ever mend?

Disappearing into the stars,

life's a warning, not out too far;

falling, farther falling,

out,

from the back of your mind,

what is this life for,

if not something more?

Myself

Lonely,

cold,

heartbroken, sick

from ancient tales told.

No mercy granted,

full gut-wrenching here.

Only by ripping

my insides out,

can I ever be whole again;

feel the everlasting

stench of the fight,

let the gutting begin,

I must bleed,

to be myself again.

Flood gates of skin, my own,

rushing free from where

once was my soul,

oh, so menacing,

these stories, take their toll.

A whore of the slave,

of the game, I once played,

trotting through fields so free,

but now I look on,

my brothers, nearly gone,

by what one may call destiny.

I won't let go, haven't a choice,

inside me, I feel,

all that I know is truth,

the shrieking malevolence

of the ancient's voice.

I must fulfill my quest,

to ever see youth,

I must bleed myself dry

again, and again,

for man's ignorance, the only sin.

I will be myself again.

No Longer Say

Smell the stench,

not breath,

garlic reek.

Her, the only one,

I seek,

one with watery leek.

Hound and hare,

always near,

stripped armor,

wound bare.

Came to me,

many a year,

where brushes grow,

edge of meadow.

This time,

I,

the guest,

to stay,

true lovers

goodbye,

no longer say.

Not Enough

All my time,

trying for the storm,

waiting for the mindlessness

of peace;

out of the flames,

ashes bore.

Questing always,

for golden fleece,

through the maze awaits, O', Minotaur.

Humans betrayed nature too long,

nature seeks to make even the score,

won by drinking and by song,

if one believes not in sin,

one can do no wrong.

In technology, unsure,

not enough tests have been run,

no time, as it were.

Ignorant, impatient humans,

need an answer so bad,

they will accept the wrong one,

if quick,

needn't make haste,

over decisions that stick.

O', can we ever win?

None care, makes bare,

they're trying to strip us of

which made man so fair,

not enough care, not enough care.

Nowhere Left

In all this mess, what's left?

Nothing to give your kids.

It's growing,

the nothing is spreading,

it's contagious;

wild, ravenous beasts,

you cannot contain us!

Doom is upon us,

in the face of diversity,

ancient madness surrounds,

death abounds.

Cancerous poisons trap us all,

the trees,

one by one,

fall.

We poor animal creatures

of the forest, fled.

What forest?

The one to the machines,

fed.

What creatures?

The hands that fed the machines?

Obscene!

Where have they fled?

Nowhere left.

Only the Ones That Knew

River dry, bloody.

Endless pain of reality.

Skeletons hold frame of existence.

Ghosts dance,

gently bow to each other

in poetic form.

The beast, awakened,

call of the wild.

Moon beckons further,

further in stride.

Lost love,

sold soul,

nothing in return.

No hand to deal,

no spirit to steal,

what more shall the creatures reveal?

Star-gazing at the sky,

what will it take?

Awake, the beast in my mind.

Falling from the sky,

I must wonder why,

if the night will ever come,

when I must say goodbye.

Told this, my life,

can't believe it's true,

my angry, tortured soul is blue.

God of ice, God of wine,

I summon something divine.

Fire burns in my eyes,

symbolize the pain,

yet, shall never feel shame.

Throw a rock, never to fall,

what will it take, to end it all?

There is no end,

I'm stuck in a circle.

Witches work in circles,

a circle of fire,

powered by desire.

Awaken,

hold me down,

prevent my fleeing.

Dance of freedom,

bewilderment achieved,

attained in the forest.

I've finally gone insane,

dancing with the beautiful nymph,

beloved trees, ever shall they be!

Who can see?

Very few.

Who can see?

Only the ones that knew.

Pollen

No one can understand this,

no matter how hard I try.

I reincarnate each morning,

after each night, I die.

No one can see my reason,

none, understand mine why.

Seasonings changing,

unnoticed by all,

even as the years pass me by.

I've become an old man,

sitting in the same spot,

repercussion of the past.

Transform, into centaur,

far away I trot.

How long is eternity?

How long will I last?

Soiled by evil seeds,

O', the spells I've cast,

days and nights ever change,

dive into the past,

all so strange.

Days of blue,

Deja-vu,

look, into the mirror,

and I ask me,

who are you?

My face has grown solemn,

as my years fade away,

my flower needs more pollen,

but there are no bees left today.

Program

They say we're not happy,

yet they took away,

abundant beautiful land,

which is sacred,

but they only say.

Why is it then,

that, each day,

from begin, to end,

these stupid pain

upon my side, do say:

'have a bright, cheery fucking day.'

Then they are the one

who take away fun,

to them,

at the cost of eternal misery.

Why are 'bad ones'

who truly love life?

All their methods,

'bullshit', says one!

'Hey, you, get over here!

Behind bars for that chum!'

At first glance, in their minds,

filth, they think,

almost half-bad

as their wretched greed wreak.

Never kill a tree, be the law,

why stupid man tears down,

each own he saw?

All these questions,

no matter,

these words I utter,

sound to them, like Mad Hatter.

Stupid ones don't perceive,

deaf unless TV does speak,

tabloids for the weak.

Rome, Burning

In a dying age,

where the future

determined by the past,

and the slow slain

by the fast,

the answers

they don't

want you to know,

futile.

In a burning Rome,

where most think

everyone believes

in a monotheistic deity

that doesn't belong.

A few years ago,

I would have been

burned alive or crucified

for saying so,

but by pure, strong will,

and the impeccable thirst

for carnal knowledge,

which drives the inner daemons

in every man

that wants goodness to prevail,

and knows deep down

this world has already

been killed,

there is a way!

Because they know

that some astronomical occurrence,

not only has to happen soon,

but is happening,

and, or, already has taken place,

and they beckon it,

for even the ignorant government

didn't expect for everything

to absolutely fall apart

as it has, no one.

It's too late,

everyone has chosen

where they stand,

deep down, they know,

that it's time for a change.

Something that will alter

the lives of our children,

whom aren't even

thought of yet,

for if this didn't happen,

neither would they,

and in a dying world,

of a dying race,

they know,

this time though

not human,

but our divine teacher,

pouring eternal light,

and infinite wisdom,

into our being.

The time is now,

there is no escaping,

the fate that has

been chosen.

It has begun,

and it has

already ended.

We have already won,

and there is nothing

any government,

or amounts of now

worthless money

can do...

It's too late!

Shedding Human Masks

Staring in the mirror

at my withered wizard face,

I know there's soon change,

flighty escape route

from this place.

Feathers sprout,

where once was flesh,

human skin,

air high in the sky,

my new home,

life to begin,

as a hawk, without sin.

Sky, the limit,

soaring to new heights,

will I die, to live again,

or snatched away?

I can sense it in the air,

a new way of living,

far fairer.

Become one with the land,

or there is no part for you.

Nature's laws of the jungle

ring true, shall see,

what justice be served,

when catastrophe

could've been avoided,

if only we had swerved.

There is no money,

no such requirement

to pass this test.

Free, sky-clad embraced,

live free, clean,

do right by Mother Earth

shan't fear no more rebirth.

Transformation,

to become myself,

stripped free, finally,

shedding human masks.

My new task unknown,

prior, to rid myself of boredom.

Sleep Again

There are some so full of sorrow,

that they never see the sun.

Been around a long, long while,

before time had begun.

Fangs are drawn again,

another destiny met.

When you found,

fateful death,

nothing better yet.

R.I.P. has no meaning

for those who stir at night,

all they know is, you look good,

your taste, splendid delight.

Ghastly eternity,

years in a flash, go by.

Nothing they would rather see,

veins pulsating vigorously.

Your heart beats, in my throat,

I can never thank enough,

for you so satisfied my hunger,

now I, no longer hurt,

sleep again, under dirt.

Sound

What secret did,

the stars, to you,

reveal?

The part of me,

once man,

under stones,

concealed.

Spirits of animals,

sacred to me, show,

the way to life and death,

my spirit,

didn't know.

Visions from beyond,

my tomb,

energy held strong,

flashes,

from before the womb,

an eternal Phoenix song,

lulling me away,

at peace, sound mind,

to try and think,

not using,

but blind;

that's when spirit kicks in,

truth

you may find.

Suspended in the Sea

Bird of prey,

in the air,

hanging,

on the brink,

of freedom's name,

as if time stops,

completely still.

Wings spread,

but no movement,

gust of wind,

suspended in the element.

Circling, but not right now,

too busy in one place,

holding up,

sea level.

Freedom,

while we still see,

birds symbolize,

in flight,

mind opened,

eternal delight.

Dancing amid stars,

suspended in the sea,

birds constantly remind us,

why they're the ones free.

Sway

This hell,

they have made,

to control us,

yet we,

the ones,

that pay,

to fund this devil,

then cry, in pain;

to repeat history

continually,

is to cast oneself insane!

The laws of Nature,

too long, forbade;

O', what sweet treasures

on this land.

Warriors, a lust for freedom,

Heathens.

Disdain for organized religion,

founding fathers had.

Powers that shouldn't be,

corrupt,

have again invaded,

from within,

businesses choke us thin,

buildings trap us in.

Their power,

to be feared,

only they say,

listen to one voice,

your own,

they again fall prey,

to their own stupid envy.

These words should be

carved in stone:

Honour

Pride

Wisdom

Self

Our founding fathers,

Lady Justice,

truth weighed,

to which side

pendulum sway?

Tender Middle

Too wild to sleep,

too tired not to dream.

Downward, spiraling,

backwaters of the mind,

we find,

as we get lost,

at the same time.

Ancient palace,

malice,

madness personified.

Through butterfly's ears,

it's heard.

Freedom.

Like screeching eagle

only can bring,

sacred flame,

Phoenix does sing.

Tender

Sacred

Naked

Freedom

The end,

of the beginning,

of the middle.

The Rest

Again, again open the drapes,

ghastly, violent, murderous rapes.

A violent murder,

without being caught,

again, a clue,

again, you sought.

Time stops,

everyone drops,

fire, falls from the sky.

Open the shade,

and begin to fall,

open the drapes,

and begin to call.

Into the night,

into the dark,

opening the blinds,

has left its mark.

Vile violence has begun,

high to the sky,

where the Phoenix sang.

A wizard on his journey, long,

a wizard on time,

and never wrong.

O', the beauty of the fire bird song.

Disappear, disappear,

into the night,

fading, fading,

out of sight.

Time has left, Winter blessed,

close the blinds,

and sleep the rest.

Rest in peace,

rest in peace,

O', benighted golden fleece.

Until the end,

a minotaur, defend.

It's my mind I want,

my mind.

The end by nine,

daughters of Zeus,

close the blinds,

close the blinds in sleep.

They're There

Here...

Cold...

Shadows around every corner, creep,

losing my mind to insanity.

Voices not silenced,

to me, loud,

are they real?

Of this, I've no doubt!

Shadow of doubt,

through the windows, out,

when cold hands are on my thigh!

I try to listen, try to hear,

stories left unsaid,

listen to their pleas,

they come to me.

Sometimes hard to figure out their plight.

Some, so young,

robbed of their life,

haunted,

every house I've owned,

just how much, the only unknown.

How many souls wander alone?

Sad,

stories untold.

Strong in stare,

intense, cold presence,

fear not,

they will come to you.

In the night,

they will seek you out,

just listen,

don't have no doubt!

Feel them moving in dark night,

hear an unknown sound,

just scarcely out of sight.

In the darkness,

they're there,

feeding on the night,

turn on a light,

you won't see them,

imagination, the only right!

Too Long Denied

Hope has fled, fearing,

life, happiness,

taken with it.

Interest not piqued,

standards not met,

on the horses, no longer a bet.

The bats, out of the cave,

the trees, don't have their way,

cut down, tons too many,

only our air source.

The Earth is killed,

painted over, branded,

ready to repackage

to the highest bidder,

sent overseas, greatest evil.

We sleep in the night,

darkness shaped sight,

cannot deny,

what you have done,

problems far worse than bombs or guns,

we've blocked out the goddamn sun!

Left to crisp,

in our poison air,

no children left,

for this pain to bear.

Grit your teeth,

hang on for the ride,

this one knocks you to the side,

for Nature, too long we've denied!

Trapped

I'm an old man,

trapped,

in a young body.

Sounds good, at first,

but I'm tired,

they want me to move.

They want change,

stuck, in a groove.

Too pushy,

I want still,

doing better,

when was ill.

My nature, patient,

make each move count!

Sense for every little thing,

yet they make no sense at all,

they see it so short,

where to me,

it's too tall.

It's got to, got to fall.

Cities overran,

in the night, by mongrels,

demon at the heart of the city,

no one in the hurry for a rescue,

gone, out of town,

singing the blues!

Wake Up

Who am I?

Gaze into mirror,

face doesn't show,

but who, none know.

Philosopher,

no longer observing,

a symbol of peace,

locked away, hate crimes,

four consecutive lifetimes.

Unjust, unruly fate,

fall on deaf ears.

Visionary, no sight left,

guru of optimism,

bereft.

Knowledge is power,

the beast will devour,

four is the number,

late, the hour.

Life, not worth living,

if not your own,

wake up, follow your star.

Let not get stale,

indulge thyself in ale!

Where

Talking to me,

from beyond,

they are!

Rattling at my door,

then silence.

Cold breath,

more than I can take.

Lights flicker on,

through the night,

gut instinct,

deep down saying,

get the fuck out!

Muster up all my courage,

feet cemented there,

against my own will,

I remain,

haunted and tormented,

continuously.

Bright gets the light,

cold the feel,

then you do know,

in darkness, they're near.

Chills, my feel,

madness, sole thought,

that I may be,

a spirit's next meal!

Where does one run,

in the night,

from the dead?

Take a left, quick,

exit my head!

Awake in your bed,

just to notice,

you were never asleep!

Get the fuck out!!!

Where???

Hate, love... fine line!

Wisdom

Death is love,

the passion,

pure,

overindulgent

initially,

to ration proper.

Deeds not judged,

solely evil, good,

do as

you know you should.

Balanced heart, mind,

along the way,

not left behind,

one, not lost,

cares not where they are.

Wisdom, patience,

knowledge,

imparted, his,

do what is right

in feeling.

Speak truth,

with open eyes,

stand up for yourself,

seek always,

to be wise.

Guide me,

whenever my time,

magic of rhythm,

poem and rhyme.

Odin, Valhalla,

live with honour, victory!

With It, You

Extreme anarchy,

in the dark,

cities burn a week.

People tired of their lives,

stand up for their rights.

How can we not see?

Clearly in plain sight.

How sickening,

disgusting, grotesque;

they have no right.

Voice of the many,

We, the People, speak

they try to crush it,

to rid of the weak.

Demolition,

destruction,

devastation,

explosions nearly wake up the heavens.

Disaster strikes,

buildings splintered,

people dead,

voices hindered.

Left and right,

no right,

both wrong.

Separated idiots,

pulling strings,

how much a puppet,

we are,

true freedom sings.

Back and forth,

to no avail,

same result,

standstill.

To overthrow,

We, the People,

with a pen flick,

in the streets,

tame the beast,

made to stick?

All false nonsense,

try to make crazy,

like them,

we have true peace,

they make no sense.

Take off wigs,

remove masks,

drop your weapons,

one on one,

let fists avail,

but you, fake,

as a computer,

technology will fail,

and with it, you!

Without a Sound

Betrayal,

strife,

away,

unkind joke,

this life.

Horror beckons me,

for I need something true,

blasphemous and murderous,

killing out of the blue.

There is no god who can save me,

I'm already underground;

like a bat at midnight,

disappearing without a sound.

Worse Before Better

Can't take anymore,

pain of living, lost it all,

kept on giving.

Prisoner to my flesh,

what an unearthly mess.

I miss my angel wings,

the sweet, soft song

the Phoenix sings,

in all his wonder, firebird.

I'm a mute,

never uttered a single word.

No blood tears could fill,

the hole in my black heart;

never afraid of the ending,

terrified from the start.

Repercussions of a life unkind,

so much magic sought.

I can't recall

why I get up at all,

why each mourning,

I get dressed,

longing to be naked

all the while.

Walking around in circles,

eternal green mile.

I never saw the day,

which would be my happiest,

the one I'd go away,

but never did I stop playing,

on and on, I play.

I really came home,

that one fateful night,

but happiness, purity,

pulled me through

without realization,

that I didn't make it at all.

Overflowing tears drowned,

where once was my heart.

Burden from birth,

tragedy from the womb.

It had to get worse,

so, I would get consumed.

Ye Who Enter

I've been absent,

from my dreams,

so long,

to me, there exists,

no right, nor wrong.

On repeat, eternally,

forever a sad,

doomed,

dark song.

Plagued by the beast,

who eradicates me.

My mind has no peace,

nor quiet,

I shall never,

in peace, rest.

Dreams,

molested,

life,

detested,

my forest lies, haunted and dead,

in,

taken,

by the cyanide, fed.

Nothing is there,

left for me,

captivated by evil tides,

no need for discretion,

no evil from me, hides.

I travel down,

on a boat,

upon which entering reads:

"Abandon all hope"

Zombie

Taken captive by my mind,

endless horrors, did I find.

First I unearthed, my mangled body,

then I ate my brains, still a slave.

Can't believe how much

they satiated the need,

for blood, and gore,

and what you can't see.

My eyes of no use,

the years of abuse

of sight.

O', if only I knew I had three,

one may have been of use to me,

but now, Greek coins cover them.

I can see for the first time again,

endless rhythm of rhyme,

stopped time.

Death's birds,

follow me in the desert,

stopping for a snack on occasion,

to which I invite, in return,

I'm granted, eternal delight

of flight.

Round and round in the sky,

my bones littered,

never returned, nor found.

I had no use for them,

I was beyond,

six feet and never looked back,

without eyes,

though nor did I look ahead,

through and through,

all of me, now dead.

Not sure why or how,

woke up in the ground,

cold, blue, and mutilated,

beyond recognition.

The only choice left,

my body's ignition.

Maybe that will get me

started again.

End Credits

Better

an open mind,

always

room left

to be filled,

than ancient tomb

closed off,

concealed, condemned!

www.ingramcontent.com/pod-product-compliance
Lightning Source LLC
Chambersburg PA
CBHW032040290426
44110CB00012B/881